Revelation›

7 messages received

What Christ expects from His Church

Revelation›

7 messages received

What Christ expects
from His Church

SELWYN HUGHES

Published by CWR, Waverley Abbey House, Waverley Lane, Farnham,
Surrey GU9 8EP

First published as *Every Day with Jesus*, September/October 1990.
This revised edition 2002.
Front cover image: CWR Creative Services

Unless otherwise indicated, all Scripture references are from the Holy Bible: New International Version (NIV), copyright © 1973, 1978, 1984 by the International Bible Society

Other Scripture quotations are marked:
Phillips: J.B. Phillips, *The New Testament in Modern English*, © 1960, 1972, J.B. Phillips, Fount Paperbacks
NKJ: *New King James Version*, © 1982, Thomas Nelson Inc.
TLB: *The Living Bible*, © 1971, 1994, Tyndale House Publishers

ISBN 1 85345 204 1
Concept development, editing, design and production by
CWR Creative Services
Printed by Omnia Books LTD.

Contents_>>

Introduction>>

I am often asked: "What is the Spirit saying to the Church of the twenty-first century?" And my reply is always this: "He is saying to the Church of this century what He said to the Church of the first century. You can read all about it in the first three chapters of the book of Revelation." Our theme for this book is based on the statement which appears seven times in the second and third chapters of Revelation: "... hear what the Spirit says to the churches." Of course, the Spirit may speak to the Church of today about matters which did not apply to the Church of the first century, but the basic issues are exactly the same as those experienced by first-century Christians. This is why I firmly believe that the three most important chapters of the Bible which the Church ought to be studying are the first three chapters of Revelation, a book many Christians fight shy of. They find it difficult to relate to its weird world of dragons, winged beasts and other strange creatures.

Perhaps this is one reason why it has become one of the most neglected books of the Bible. Something is said of it, however, that is not said of any other book in the Bible – that those who read it and take note of its words are guaranteed a special blessing from the Lord (1:3).

No other book has encouraged and challenged the people of God throughout the centuries like the book of Revelation. And if, as someone has said, "the soul grows by a series of challenges", then our study could mark a significant spiritual development both in you and in the church where God has placed you.

The_revelation_of_Jesus_Christ_>> 1

Revelation 1:1–20

"Blessed is the one who
reads the words of this
prophecy, and ... those who
hear it and take to heart
what is written in it ..."
(Revelation 1:3)

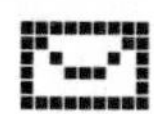

The book of Revelation begins by describing itself as "The revelation of Jesus Christ". Sometimes Christians refer to it as "The revelation of John" but this is incorrect. The revelation is, of course, given to John, but is of Jesus Christ.

Is this not precisely what the Church needs at every moment of its perilous existence – a vision of the transcendent and glorious Christ? Moral exhortations and pious entreaties all have their place, of course, in the Church's development and growth, but the people of God, set as they are in the midst of a hostile environment, need constantly to fix their gaze upon the fact that Jesus Christ is Lord. Theologians who systematically set about mutilating the Person of Christ and denying His deity cause more harm than they realise, for the Church rises and falls in relation to its concept of Christ. "A church with its back to the wall, fighting for survival," says John Stott, "must see Christ."

This is exactly what happens when we read the book of Revelation – we gain a clearer view of Him. This revelation (or unveiling) of Christ's glory is said, in the opening verse of chapter 1, to be given by God – "The revelation of Jesus Christ, which God gave him ..." Elsewhere in the New Testament Jesus reveals God: "Anyone who has seen me has seen the Father" (John 14:9). Now, however, the roles are reversed. It is God who reveals Jesus! This is a fulfilment of the law which Jesus expounded: "For whoever wants to save his life will lose it, but whoever loses his life for me will save it" (Luke 9:24). Jesus lost His life in revealing the Father, and found it again in the Father's revealing of Him.

⟨The King of kings⟩

We said that no one can read the book of Revelation without gaining a clearer view of Jesus Christ and verse 5 of chapter 1 puts this very clearly: "… and from Jesus Christ, who is the faithful witness, the firstborn from the dead, and the ruler of the kings of the earth." Here Christ is given three impressive titles.

He is the *faithful witness.* Is is not the main function of the Church to bear witness to the world? Then let it take its example from its risen and glorified Lord who, during His ministry here on earth, never faltered in His presentation of God's truth.

He is called also the *firstborn from the dead.* In John 3:16 Christ is spoken of as the "one and only Son". This means that He stands unrivalled and supreme. No one can stand with Him or equal Him. As firstborn from the dead He is the first of an order which others can follow. If Christ, for example, had ascended into heaven from the Mount of Transfiguration, there would have been no way by which we could have followed Him. By going through death, however, and then rising from the dead, He has made it gloriously possible for those who trust Him to follow the pathway He has made into heaven.

The third title He is given is the *ruler of the kings of the earth.* A church which is facing persecution and ostracism urgently needs this revelation. Earthly kings may work against us, but Christ is the King of kings.

⟨This Man loved me⟩

Consideration of Christ's supremacy and glory leads inevitably to heartfelt praise and worship. Is it any wonder that John, after contemplating the titles of his Lord, breaks forth into the glorious doxology of Revelation 1:4–6? W.S. Landor, in a compelling and beautiful poem, tells of a sick and dying man writing to his lover reminding her that, after his death, the letters he wrote would bring home to her heart the full depth of his love:

 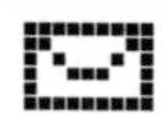

> Resting on one white hand a warm wet cheek,
> Over my open volume you will say,
> "This man loved me!" then rise and trip away.

As John reflects on the wonder of his Lord, he comes to the same conclusion. "This Man loved me!" he cries. But he does not rise and trip away. He stays to worship and adore.

"To him who loves us ..." writes John (Rev. 1:5). This is the essence of Christianity. The reason why we love Christ is because He first loved us. "He did the courting," as one old saintly Scottish woman put it. But more than that, says John, He "has freed us ..." (1:5). John rejoiced in the fact (as do all Christians) that first we are saved from the penalty of sin and then Christ goes on to save us from its power.

However, there is still more to come. He "has made us to be a kingdom and priests to serve his God and Father" (1:6). As kings, we are expected to reign over sin, self and the world. As priests, we are to bear the sorrows of the world and carry them into Christ's presence by fervent, believing, intercessory prayer.

⟨A trilogy of triumph⟩

He who has redeemed us and made us kings and priests is one day coming to establish His rule and reign throughout the universe. It is fitting, therefore, that Christ is now introduced to John as "the Alpha and the Omega" (1:8). As you know, *alpha* is the first letter of the Greek alphabet and *omega* the last. These words are simply saying that Christ is the cosmic Alphabet out of which God frames all His transactions with the universe. Christ not only began the universe, but will speak its final word.

The John writing here is John the apostle, son of Zebedee and brother of James. He is believed to have survived the other apostles and to have lived to a ripe old age as leader of the church at Ephesus, prior to his imprisonment on the isle of Patmos. His relationship to the seven churches of Asia (which he must have known intimately) is made all the closer by their mutual suffering. He says, "I, John, your brother and companion in the suffering and kingdom and patient endurance that are ours in Jesus ..." (1:9).

Notice the words – "suffering", "kingdom" and "patient endurance". The trilogy is impressive and important. "Suffering" – that is what hits them first. Then "kingdom" – no matter what persecution may come, the kingdom is beneath their feet. Standing on solid ground they can, therefore, face everything that comes with "patient endurance". Someone has described this as a "trilogy of triumph". No matter what the world may throw at us, our feet are firmly established in the kingdom of our God. We may often tremble on that Rock, but the Rock will never tremble under us.

<The divine masterpiece>

John is now instructed to write what he sees on a scroll and send it to the seven churches in Asia (1:11). In a vision, he sees seven golden lampstands (1:12) and in the midst of them stands the exalted Christ, with seven stars in His right hand (1:16). The seven lampstands are explained as the seven churches of Asia, and the seven stars as the messengers (or presiding elders) of those churches (1:20). Thus, not only is Christ seen to be radiant, but His churches are also filled with light. In every age the Church of Jesus Christ is expected to be a light-bearer and to shine out in the midst of the world's darkness. It can only do so, however, as it stays close to Him.

What Christ expects of His Church, and what He has to say to

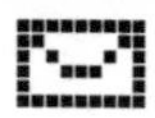

His people, we shall discover in more detail as we go on, but let us pause for a moment to emphasise the fact that the Church is not yours or mine – it is His. He regards it as His most precious possession. It is, as someone called it, "the Divine Masterpiece", far outweighing and outshining every other act of creation. He walks in the midst of it, knows everything there is to know about it and cares for it with a love that conquers all hostility and overwhelms all suspicion and distrust. Remember, however, that the Church is a fellowship around Christ – not ourselves. If we become the centre, then the light turns to darkness.

{Local – or universal?}

Before we go on to consider in detail the message of Christ to the seven churches in Asia, the question must be asked: Do these letters have only a special and local significance, or have they something to say to the Church of this present century? I believe with all my heart that Christ's letters to those first-century Christians in Asia Minor (now known as Turkey) have a permanent and universal application to the Church at all times.

Commentators have pointed out that the three main tactics of the devil – persecution, error and sin – are just as evident in the Church of today as they were in the midst of those first-century Christian communities. As we take a global view of the Church at this present moment and let our gaze sweep across the continents, we see that in some parts of the world the Church is faced with severe physical persecution, while in other parts the Church is locked in combat with materialist ideologies and all kinds of heresies. Almost everywhere the Church struggles against a lowering of moral standards as the world seeks to entice the people of God to conform to its own ways.

The book of Revelation can be understood only when it is seen as God's message to His people in this situation. God has put the Church in the world and the devil is seeking to put the world in the Church. Christ expects us to resist the devil's enticements, and in each of the seven letters that follow, He gives us key words which, put together, constitute a picture of what He truly expects of His Church.

⟨Further Study⟩

John 13:1, 15:1–9, 15:13; 1 John 3:16

1. How does Jesus love us?
2. How do we perceive the love of God?

Eph. 1:1–23, 4:15, 5:23–25; Col. 1:18, 2:19

3. What is Christ's position in the Church?
4. What is He to have in all things?

Zech. 3:1; Eph. 4:27, 6:11; James 4:7; 1 Pet. 5:1–8

5. What are we to be?
6. How are we to deal with Satan's attempts to entice us?

The_letter_to_the_church_at Ephesus,_"The divine Overseer"_>>

Revelation 2:1–7

"Write a letter to the leader of the church at Ephesus and tell him this: 'I write to inform you of a message from him who walks among the churches ...'"
(Revelation 2:1, TLB)

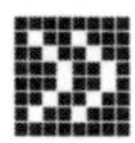

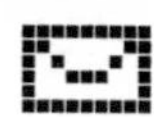

We turn now to look at the first of Christ's letters to the seven churches of Asia – the letter addressed to the church in Ephesus. There is a good deal of speculation among Christian teachers as to why this particular church should be the subject of Christ's first address. Some view the message to the seven churches as covering seven distinct periods of time, from the birth of the Church at Pentecost up to the second coming of Christ. Others claim the messages are given in order of priority – love being the foremost quality Christ expects of His Church.

I suspect, however, that the real reason is not dispensational but geographical. It has been pointed out that if a postman were to deliver these letters by hand to the seven churches in Asia, the route he would have followed from Patmos would start with Ephesus, then move on to Smyrna, Pergamum, Thyatira, Sardis, Philadelphia and finally Laodicea.

It becomes clear from the opening verses of this letter that Christ is not a mere bystander in the affairs of His Church, but is the divine Overseer of His people: "These are the words of him who ... walks among the seven golden lampstands" (2:1). How desperately we need to catch a fresh vision of our risen Lord standing in the midst of His Church. It must be remembered that what binds all believers together is not that we subscribe to a common creed, but the thrilling truth that the risen Christ stands among us.

‹Christ's commendation›

In all but one of the seven letters we are considering, Christ passes on criticism and condemnation in varying degrees; to the church in Smyrna alone, He gives unrestricted praise. To the church in Laodicea He gives unrestricted condemnation; the church in Philadelphia comes in for considerably more praise than blame; and the church in Sardis receives more blame. The letters to Pergamum and Thyatira (as well as this first one to Ephesus) contain varying degrees of approval and disapproval.

At the beginning of each of the seven letters, Christ announces Himself by one or more of the features contained in the titles given to Him in the first chapter.

The letter to Ephesus can be divided into three sections. It begins with a commendation, moves into condemnation and closes with a command. First, the commendation: "I know your deeds, your hard work and your perseverance. I know that you cannot tolerate wicked men ..." (2:2). Of course Christ knows; He said, "For where two or three come together in my name, there am I with them" (Matt. 18:20). It is Christ at the centre of His Church who prevents its dissolution and disintegration in a world which constantly threatens to engulf it.

Christ commends them for three things: first, their hard work, "toiling to the point of exhaustion" (from the Greek); second, their perseverance; third, their orthodoxy. The Ephesian Christians were hard working in their service, determined in their commitment and orthodox in their doctrine. What a magnificent model of a church! The church in Ephesus was highly commended by the Lord Jesus Christ. They stood firm in the midst of persecution and, although faced with serious false teaching, they had remained undeceived.

Yet in spite of these fine qualities, something was missing. They had left their first love.

<Christ's condemnation>

It is this which brings a strong condemnation from the lips of the Lord Jesus Christ: "Yet I hold this against you: You have forsaken your first love" (2:4). Somehow they had allowed their love for Christ to cool. They had fallen away from their first love and, despite the efficiency of their service, the blamelessness of their character and the orthodoxy of their doctrine, they were backslidden people.

Their love had chilled. This describes so many nowadays who, caught up in their activity for Christ, have lost that inner glow which once burned through every fibre of their being? Can we honestly say that we are as much in love with the Lord today as when we first came to know Him? Do we get up each morning, look into His face and are thrilled with the wonder of His love in our hearts?

Some Christians respond to this challenge by saying, "But my love for Christ has matured and found new ways of expression." It is good when love develops and matures, but take care that this attitude is not a rationalisation.

<Christ's command>

Efficiency of service, blamelessness of character and orthodoxy of doctrine are but ashes on a rusty altar if we know nothing of a burning, blazing, passionate and romantic love for the Lord Jesus Christ. How can this sad state of affairs be corrected? The solution comes in the form of a command, "Remember the height from which you have fallen! Repent and do the things you did at first ..." (2:5) – remember, repent and return.

There are times when a backward look can be sinful, and there are times when it can be wise. To look back with longing eyes, as did Lot's wife to the sinful lifestyle of Sodom from which she had been saved, is to invite disaster. But to look back with the precious gift of memory to discover how and why we have descended from the spiritual heights we once occupied is something that occasionally every Christian ought to do.

I have mentioned before that in every case in which I have counselled someone over the question of having left their first love, I have found that the cause lies in a wrong action, a wrong attitude or a wrong word. They did something, said something or perhaps omitted to do something they should have done, and as a result their spiritual life became chilled. If, as you read these lines, you are conscious of having left your first love then, with God's help, reflect upon your past. Where did you go wrong? Was it something you said or did that has never been put right? Bring it into spiritual focus now, for you cannot begin to deal with it until you first begin to recognise it.

⟨Repent⟩

Jesus' command to the church in Ephesus, "Remember the height from which you have fallen! Repent and do the things you did at first" (2:5), has been described by someone as "the three R's" – remember, repent and return. Once we have discovered the cause of our waning love (remembered something in our past that was not dealt with in an appropriate way), then we must move on to the next step and repent.

What is repentance? "It is a change of mind," says one famous preacher, "leading to a change of direction." It is an action of the will by which we turn our back on all known sin. One of the greatest mistakes we Christians can make is to think that an emotional upheaval has to take place inside us before we can repent. It is this wrong belief which is keeping the Church in Britain (and in some other parts of the world) from experiencing real revival.

Repentance, I say again, is an act of the will. Christ did not entreat the Ephesian Christians to feel badly about their sins. It

is not so much what they felt about them, but what they did about them, that would bring them back to their first love. If we delay putting things right and asking God's forgiveness for the ways in which we have hurt Him, simply because we don't feel like doing it, then we may well wait a lifetime. If we have sinned against God in any way, then we must ask His forgiveness and put things right. The same principle applies to others we may have wronged or hurt. There is no need to wait a moment longer. Let's examine our lives right now in His burning presence and get rid of everything that divides our loyalty to Him.

⟨Return⟩

The third of "the three R's" by which we are brought into a restored relationship with Jesus Christ is "return". Christ says, "... do the things you did at first. If you do not repent, I will come to you and remove your lampstand from its place" (2:5). There is no suggestion that having fallen out of love they must wait until they have fallen in love with Him again. There is no need for any further waiting – they must resume the works they used to do.

What are these "works" of which Christ speaks? Well, we know that the Ephesian church was a veritable hive of industry for, as we have seen, Christ speaks of them as "toiling to the point of exhaustion". So His words could not have meant that they must work any harder. I suspect that the "works" He was referring to here were the works that were necessary for the building up of their own personal relationship with Him – the daily Quiet Time, personal prayer and meditation in His Word. It was here that the rot had set in. They had neglected to feed their love for Christ by their daily devotions and although they were seen to be busy and industrious in their corporate activity, they were spiritually beggared and bankrupt because of this failure to cultivate their own individual relationship with the Lord.

Is this not exactly where much of the spiritual bankruptcy of the twenty-first-century Church lies? We must give Christ the same amount of time in prayer and daily devotion that we gave Him when we first came to know Him.

⟨A warning and a promise⟩

The letter to the church at Ephesus closes with both a solemn warning and a gracious promise. Christ warns them that if they fail to obey His commands, then their ministry will be terminated: "If you do not repent, I will come to you and remove your lampstand from its place" (2:5). We must remember that the Church is continuously on trial. Its presence and ministry in the world is secure only as long as it relates to Christ.

I will never forget standing with a group of Christians on the site of what was once the city of Ephesus. Even though it is now in ruins, it is still a breathtaking spectacle. Yet there is no sign of a Christian church anywhere in the vicinity. Did Christ's warning take effect there? I believe it did. The Ephesus church failed to obey His command and, in consequence, its light was extinguished. A church has no light without love. It can maintain a building and support a minister, but if there is no love there can be no light. The lampstand has been removed.

But to the warning Christ adds a glorious promise: "To him who overcomes, I will give the right to eat from the tree of life, which is in the paradise of God" (2:7). Each of the seven letters ends with a promise to the overcomer. In this case, it is free access to the tree of life in God's eternal paradise. The true Christian is destined for heaven, so no matter how dark and gloomy life may become on this earth, the true Christian is not shaken. This world is not our home – we are only passing

through and the reward of loving is to know love in all its fullness in the perfect atmosphere of a future heaven.

⟨Further study⟩

Gal. 6:9–10; James 5:1–11; Heb. 12:1

1. What are we not to become?
2. How are we to run the race?

Psa. 39:3; Jer. 20:9; Luke 24:13–35

3. Why were the two disciples disconsolate?
4. What caused their hearts to burn again?

1 John 5:4; Rev. 3:1–22, 21:7

5. What does God promise to the overcomer?
6. What is the victory that overcomes the world?

The_letter_to_the_church_at Smyrna,_"The_evidence_of_love"_>>

Revelation 2:8–11

"To the angel of the church in Smyrna write: These are the words of him who is the First and the Last ..."
(Revelation 2:8)

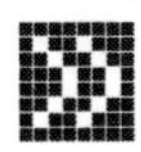

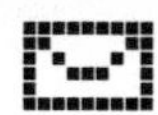

We turn now to the second of the letters to the seven churches – the letter addressed to the church in Smyrna. Earlier we said that each of the seven churches has a significant key-word, in itself a mark of a true and living church. We saw that the letter to the church in Ephesus underlined the significance of love. Without love the Church is without light and no matter what other qualities it possesses, if there is an absence of love then it is beggared, bankrupt and broken.

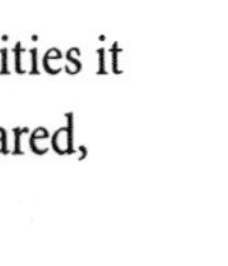

If love is the first quality which Christ expects to see in His Church – then what is the second? It is this – suffering. Before examining this word in detail, let's bring into focus the physical details of the church in Smyrna.

The city lay about 60 miles north of Ephesus, and would be the next city to which our imaginary postman would come were he to deliver the letters personally. Smyrna, at the time this letter was given, was the pride of all Asia. It is, in fact, the only city of all the seven churches which is still thriving and is called at the present time, Izmir. We do not know how the church at Smyrna was founded, but we can conclude from Acts 19:10 that Paul's ministry at Ephesus influenced, to some degree at least, the founding of a Christian church in this city.

The church in Smyrna experienced persecution and suffering to a degree that none of the other churches had to bear. It is a fact that many of us will tend to shy away from, but suffering is a natural consequence of love. If our love is genuine and true then we will be willing to suffer for it.

‹The cosmic guarantee›

Christ starts His letter to the church in Smyrna by focusing their attention on Himself: "These are the words of him who is the First and the Last, who died and came to life again" (2:8). This is always the way our Lord seeks to comfort His people in times of persecution and distress. He does not attempt to lecture them or exhort them, without first revealing Himself. He therefore quietly assumes the divine titles which He previously revealed in the first chapter of the book. Let the wonder of these thrilling words sink deep into your heart right now – Christ is the First and the Last, and He who died is alive again.

A great philosopher once said, "The religion that will conquer the world must have a cosmic guarantee." This is precisely what Christ gives us in these immortal words – a cosmic guarantee. A man, lost in a trackless jungle, asked a native if he could show him the way. The native obliged, but as they trudged through the dense forest, the man became doubtful about his guide and asked, "Is this really the way?" The native replied, "There is no way. I am the way." His shrewdness brought the man safely through that jungle even though there was no way – the native was the way.

In the midst of a trackless universe Jesus Christ alone is the Way. He is the Way backwards as well as the Way forwards. There is no adequate solution to the past or the future without Him. Wherever we go in life, we meet Christ – coming or going.

‹Christ – or Caesar?›

Christ addresses each of the seven churches with the phrase, "I know", and in the case of Smyrna He begins by saying, "I know your afflictions and your poverty" (2:9). In this phrase, Christ speaks directly to the needs of His readers showing them that He is not unmindful of their particular problems, and is indeed acutely aware of the tribulation through which they are passing.

Clearly, in the case of the church at Smyrna, the affliction was

 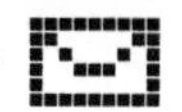

suffering. It wasn't an easy thing to be a Christian in Smyrna. The city had acquired a reputation for loyalty to the Roman Empire, and as a result a temple had been erected in the city to the Emperor Tiberius. Citizens were required to sprinkle incense on the fire that burned before his bust and acknowledge him, Caesar, to be Lord. Christians who would not conform were outlawed and persecuted. This is why Christ says, "I know ... your poverty ... I know the slander of those who say they are Jews and are not ..." (2:9).

The poverty came about because of the refusal on the part of Smyrna's citizens to trade or do business with the Christians, and the slander came from the Jewish community who, according to Christ's own words, were nothing more than "a synagogue of Satan" (2:9). Poverty and slander was the price they had to pay for their unwillingness to compromise. It cost something to be a Christian in Smyrna.

‹"He has done me no wrong"›

But there was worse to come. "Do not be afraid of what you are about to suffer. I tell you, the devil will put some of you in prison to test you, and you will suffer persecution for ten days. Be faithful, even to the point of death" (2:10). Persecution, imprisonment and even death, are now a real possibility, says the exalted Christ.

One of the men who must have heard that statement being read out in the church in Smyrna was a young man by the name of Polycarp. He is one of the best-known Christian martyrs and was a native of Smyrna. These words may well have been a great source of strength to him in later years, for history records that in AD 156 he was hunted down and dragged into the amphitheatre in Smyrna to face the proconsul, who challenged him to "swear by the genius of Caesar, and to revile the Christ". Polycarp replied in words that have been quoted in sermons and writings down through the centuries: "Eighty and six years have I served Him, and He has done me no wrong; how then can I blaspheme my King who saved me?" He was then taken and burned at the stake, but the wind blew the flames away from him, so a soldier's sword finally ended his life.

Make no mistake about it, wherever Christ's Church sets its face to stand uncompromisingly against the world, then suffering is the inevitable result. For many Christians living in the twenty-first century, it may not mean martyrdom, but it may involve us in much suffering.

‹"Little in us to hate"›

Some Christians, I know, will shy away from the subject of suffering and turn to less challenging matters but, quite simply, the truth is that we are not worthy to be called Christ's disciples unless we are willing to come to terms with this all-important issue.

Someone once asked me: "Why is it that the Church here in the West does not seem to suffer in the way that it does in other parts of the world?" As I pondered that question, I was driven to the conclusion that one of the main reasons is because it has (generally speaking) compromised its testimony. Let's face it – there is really little difference between us and the world. The clear lines of demarcation which ought to exist between the Church and secular society are blurred and indistinct. Our moral standards are not all that much higher than the world's. Our personal lives do not challenge unbelievers; we are so much like them that they find little or nothing in us to hate.

Of course, there are exceptions to this generalisation, yet it

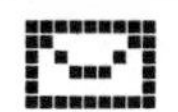

must still be accepted that the Church here in the West is making little impact upon the society in which it lives. We seldom speak out with one voice against sin, evil and corruption, impurity, pornography, unrestricted abortion and other vital social issues. We prefer to leave it to individuals to campaign against these issues, while we, as one writer says, “tread more delicately than Agag in our anxiety not to step on anybody’s corns” (see 1 Sam. 15:32).

<“Outside the camp”>

Take, for example, the messages preached from our pulpits. Although, again, there are noticeable exceptions, by far the majority fail to deal with the majestic themes of Scripture such as original sin, the judgment of God and the atoning death of Jesus Christ. Thousands who attend our churches week by week are ignorant of these truths because they are never properly presented. Instead, many congregations are subjected to entertaining sermons and talks that bear little or no relation to their needs.

Then what about some of the Church’s methods? Take as an example the indiscriminate baptism of infants. John Stott says of the Church of England, “Our ranks are filled with baptised unbelievers.” He goes on to say, “Can it ever be justifiable to baptise, into Christ and His Church, children who have neither parents nor grandparents who profess the Christian faith? Christian conscience can only reply to this question with a downright ‘No’.”

What would happen if, in the next few weeks, the Church were to act as one in preaching Christ’s truth and refused to go along with the world in things we know are not right? I will tell you what would happen. Our uncompromising stand would bring us to the place described in Hebrews 13:13: "Let us, then, go to him outside the camp, bearing the disgrace he bore." It is the place where the Church should always be – outside the camp, bearing His reproach. And that could be the greatest thing that could ever happen to us.

‹Live well and die well›

The letter to Smyrna ends with a glorious promise: "Be faithful, even to the point of death, and I will give you the crown of life" (2:10). "He who overcomes will not be hurt at all by the second death" (2:11).

Many crowns are spoken of in Scripture. There is the crown of gold which is the symbol of steadfastness (Rev. 4:4). There is the crown that will last forever, the symbol of perseverance (1 Cor. 9:25–27). There is the crown of righteousness which is the symbol of devotion and loyalty to Christ (2 Tim. 4:8–10). There is the crown of rejoicing, the soul-winner's crown (1 Thess. 2:19–20). There is the crown of glory, the shepherd's crown given to those who have been involved in the care of Christ's sheep (1 Pet. 5:1–4). Then, here in Revelation 2:10, there is the crown of life for those who have suffered and given their lives for the cause of the gospel.

In the letter to Ephesus, the overcomer's reward was to eat of the tree of life (Rev. 2:7). Here the symbol is changed – it is now a crown of life. To the Christians in Ephesus the symbol of the tree of life was more appropriate as love was their chief need. The love they had for Christ was dying within them and they needed to be reconnected to the life that is love. Here, however, the suffering Christians of Smyrna needed a new vision, not of a tree, but of a winning post. They are told that though they may not escape sudden death, they will certainly not be overcome by

the "second death" (Rev. 2:11; 20:6).

To those who have to suffer and perhaps give their lives because of an uncompromising stand, the assurance is this: Christ knows everything, and one day He will meet them personally at the doors of eternity to present them with a crown of life.

‹Further study›

Matt. 5:11–16; Acts 5:17–42

1. When are we to rejoice and be glad?

2. In what did the early apostles rejoice?

Rom. 8:17; Heb. 11:25; 1 Pet. 2:20; 1 Pet. 5:1–10

3. What comes through suffering?

4. Do you ever suffer for righteousness' sake?

1 Cor. 9:25; 2 Tim. 2:1–13; Rev. 4:10

5. What is the promise to those who suffer with Him?

6. What sort of crown do we obtain?

The_letter_to_the_church_at Pergamum,_"The_biblical_balance"_››

Revelation 2:12–17

"To the angel of the church
in Pergamum write ..."
(Revelation 2:12)

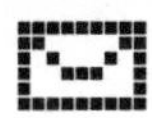

We continue following the journey of an imaginary postman in his delivery of the letters to the seven churches of Asia, and the next stop on our route is the church in Pergamum. The city lay about 60 miles north of Smyrna and at the time these letters were written it was known to be a strong centre of paganism and idolatry. Two of the main deities honoured there (amongst hundreds of others) were Dionysos and Asklepios – the gods of healing. The historian R.H. Charles describes Pergamum as "the Lourdes of the province of Asia and the seat of a famous school of medicine". One writer says, "In Pergamum it was not so much Christ who was evident – but antichrist."

If to the church in Ephesus Christ's chief word was love, and to Smyrna suffering, what was His word to the church in Pergamum? It was this – truth. The conflict in Pergamum was not so much between good and evil (although, of course, it was that) as between truth and error.

In His customary way, Christ begins with a revelation of who He is – "These are the words of him who has the sharp, double-edged sword" (2:12). In the opening words of this letter Christ reassures the Christians in Pergamum by stating that He is well-equipped to handle the forces of darkness and error. His word of truth is well able to defeat and overcome error. The epistle to the Hebrews refers to God's Word as a two-edged sword (Heb. 4:12) and Augustine said, "The two edges were the Old and New Testaments, and one needs both in order to overcome the enemy."

⟨A right balance⟩

Christ is concerned not only that we love Him and suffer for Him, but also that we hold the truth for Him. Mark this, and mark it well – Christ is deeply and passionately concerned for truth. There were those in the Church of the first century, as there are those today, who would argue that we should drown all our doctrinal differences in the ocean of love. "If we love each other," they say, "truly love each other, then what does it matter what we believe?"

E. Stanley Jones says, in one of his books, "The truth must be approached in a spirit of love, but truth must not be sacrificed for the sake of love." We have all met those Christians who are so zealous for truth that they become harsh and abrasive in their attitudes. But we have also all met those Christians who are so "loving" in their approach that truth becomes unimportant.

The proper Christian attitude lies right between the two. Without truth, love becomes sloppy and sentimental; without love, truth becomes harsh, bitter and abrasive. Christ promised His disciples that if they continued in His Word they would know the truth and the truth would set them free (John 8:32). We must maintain a biblical balance so that we always hold the truth in love and love others in the truth and grow, not only in love, but in our ability to discern and recognise error/fallacy/untruth.

‹Error – often of satanic origin›

In the letter to the church at Pergamum, as in the previous letters, Christ makes it clear that He knows even the tiniest detail of the lives of His readers. In Ephesus, His knowledge extended to the works His people did and in Smyrna, to the persecution they endured. Here, it includes the environment in which they lived. "I know where you live – where Satan has his throne ..." (2:13).

Yet again Christ speaks a word that is directly related to their personal need. He stresses the fact that He knows what they are going through and that they were carrying out their worship

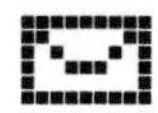

and witness in the very city where Satan had decided to set up his throne. In this one sentence, Christ cuts through the dense fog of error that surrounds them and exposes the source of that error – Satan himself. Let us make no mistake about this – Satan is the source of the false teaching to which the Church is constantly exposed.

Pergamum now lies in ruins, but the arch-deceiver, who inveigled the people of that day into worshipping non-existent deities, is still amongst us. We in the Western Church may not face physical persecution in the way that our brethren do in other lands, but we are being beset by the severe storms of theological change. Error is quietly creeping into the Church of the twenty-first century. The only direction left open to us is heavenward. Can we get enough inspiration from that source to resist these satanic attacks?

‹The doctrine of Balaam›

Although many in the church at Pergamum were holding tight to the truth of the gospel, others had drifted from it and were entertaining false teaching. Christ describes it as "the teaching of Balaam, who taught Balak to entice the Israelites to sin ..." and "the teaching of the Nicolaitans" (Rev. 2:14–15). Most scholars agree that the doctrine of Balaam and the doctrine of the Nicolaitans were one and the same thing.

The story of Balaam is recorded for us in Numbers 22–24. It tells of how Balaam, a prophet of the Almighty, was enticed by Balak, king of Moab, to curse the tribes of Israel who were about to cross the River Jordan and enter the promised land. However, every time Balaam opened his mouth to curse Israel, God moved him to speak words of blessing. Frustrated by this, Balaam suggested to King Balak that he should arrange for the Moabite girls to seduce the men of Israel by inviting them to take part in immoral and idolatrous feasts. He knew, of course, that such behaviour would bring down on them the anger of God.

What Balaam was to ancient Israel, the Nicolaitans were to the church in Pergamum. "Christ has redeemed us from the law," they reasoned, "so we are no longer under law but under grace." This teaching, still present in some parts of the Church, says, "Sin is only a worry for the unbeliever. We are free to do what we like, for the more we sin, the more God can show us how gracious and forgiving He is." What does Christ think of such behaviour? He says quite clearly, "Repent, therefore!" (Rev. 2:16). God does not condemn sin in the sinner in order to condone it in the saint.

⟨No compromise with error⟩

We now have to ask ourselves a direct question: How does Christ view a church that has allowed itself to be overtaken by error? He expects it to repent (Rev. 2:16).

The challenge that rang out in the midst of the church in Pergamum is ringing just as clearly in the Church of today: "He who has an ear, let him hear what the Spirit says to the churches" (2:17). If we allow error to creep into the Church unchallenged and unresisted, then a good deal of the blame must lie at our own door. We each need to ask ourselves today: "Am I allowing error to be propagated in my church unchallenged?" Some of you, of course, worship in churches where every week the truth is gloriously proclaimed. If this is so, then thank God for it. Others, however, listen to sermons Sunday after Sunday in which Christ's deity is denied and where the robe of truth is deliberately and systematically dragged into the mud of false teaching.

 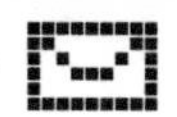

If you have allowed this to take place without firm and loving resistance, then Christ's word to you is quite clear: "Repent!" Does it mean nothing to you that Christ's Name is being denied and that His gospel is being dishonoured? "Repent therefore!" (2:16). Truth cannot be compromised. There are many things about which we can agree to differ in relation to the Bible, but on the issue of Christ's divinity, there is no room for negotiation or appeasement. We must understand that the source of such error is not merely human but satanic. Anyone who climbs into a pulpit in order to deny Christ's deity is not an ambassador of Christ but an agent of the devil.

‹The sword of the Lord›

Having called upon the church at Pergamum to repent, Christ now shares with them what will happen if the grievous error is not rooted out: "Otherwise, I will soon come to you and will fight against them with the sword of my mouth" (2:16). You may remember that in the vision John described in the first chapter of Revelation, Christ was seen as the Word of God with a sharp two-edged sword coming out of His mouth (1:16). Just as Balaam was killed with a sword (Num. 31:8, Josh. 13:22) so the power of God's Word would overcome the unrepentant false teachers in Pergamum, and bring them under condemnation and judgment.

The Word of God, which saves those who obey it, also destroys those who disobey it. The saving Word, if rejected, becomes a searing Word that is sharp and powerful and swiftly destroys the unrepentant. Our task is to resist error; it is Christ's task to overcome it; this is why we need do no more than quietly, lovingly and firmly set our face against it.

This does not mean, of course, that denominations who have teachers and ministers who openly teach untruth, must not act to remove them from their midst. Once we have acted, however, we must not continue criticising and vilifing them for they will be dealt with firmly and definitely by the divine Executioner. We must make sure that hatred of error does not lead to hatred of persons.

‹A new name›

Christ closes His letter to the church in Pergamum with the promise of an eternal reward: "To him who overcomes, I will give some of the hidden manna. I will also give him a white stone with a new name written on it, known only to him who receives it" (2:17). The hidden manna alludes, no doubt, to the manna that was kept in the ark of the covenant as a symbol of God's provision for the children of Israel in the wilderness (Exod. 16:32–35; Heb. 9:4). Christ is our hidden manna, unseen to human eyes, but an ever-present reality to the eye of faith. When we close our eyes in death we shall open them again in eternity to gaze upon our hidden manna, the Lord Jesus Christ.

The white stone refers (in my opinion) to the custom prevailing at that time among young men about to go to war. Aware of the fact that they might not see each other until they were much older, they would break open a white stone, write their name on one half, then exchange stones so that they carried each other's name with them throughout the battles. Later, when time had taken its toll of their physical features, those two stones would, in many cases, be the means of establishing their identities.

The white stone given to the one who overcomes will have "a new name written on it" (2:17). This is a pledge that our

individuality will remain intact. We shall not be lost among the multitude of the redeemed. We shall bear a name – a new name – that will sum up (as Christ's Name does for Him) the uniqueness of our personalities which the grace of God has produced and realised.

⟨Further study⟩

John 1:14, 14:6; Eph. 4:1–16

1. How would you define truth?
2. How are we to share the truth?

Jer. 5:1–14, 23:29; Eph. 6:17; Heb. 4:12

3. What are some of the descriptions of God's Word?
4. What are some of its effects?

Zeph. 3:20; Luke 10:1–20; Phil. 3:20; Heb. 12:22–23

5. What are we to rejoice in?
6. Where is our citizenship?

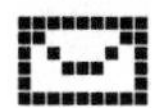

The_letter_to_the_church_at Thyatira,_"Who_may_ascend_the hill_of_the_Lord?"_››

Revelation 2:18–29

"To the angel of the church in Thyatira write: These are the words of the Son of God, whose eyes are like blazing fire and whose feet are like burnished bronze." *(Revelation 2:18)*

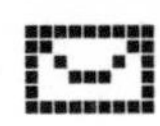

As we continue our journey along the great circular road that linked the seven cities in the province of Asia, we come to the city of Thyatira. Here a fine Christian church flourished in which the four qualities of love, faith, patience and service appeared to blossom, as in a beautiful garden. The city itself was prosperous and was recognised as being more of a commercial centre than a political one. It was famous throughout the whole of Asia (and further afield) for its special purple dye. Lydia, the first convert in Europe, whose heart the Lord opened at Philippi, was a native of Thyatira (Acts 16:14). She had doubtless journeyed to Philippi for the purpose of trading in this special and unique commodity.

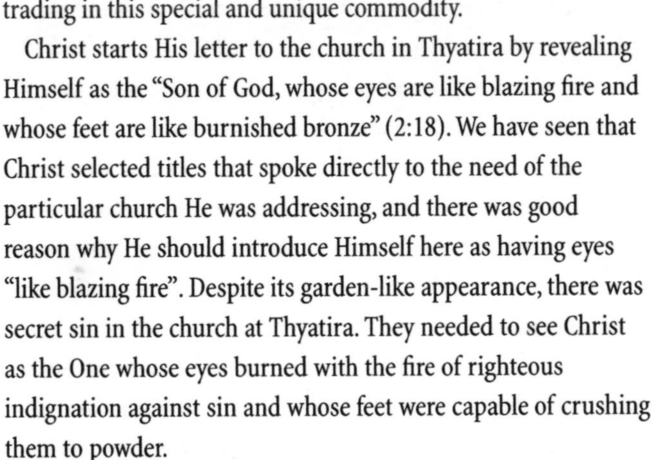

Christ starts His letter to the church in Thyatira by revealing Himself as the "Son of God, whose eyes are like blazing fire and whose feet are like burnished bronze" (2:18). We have seen that Christ selected titles that spoke directly to the need of the particular church He was addressing, and there was good reason why He should introduce Himself here as having eyes "like blazing fire". Despite its garden-like appearance, there was secret sin in the church at Thyatira. They needed to see Christ as the One whose eyes burned with the fire of righteous indignation against sin and whose feet were capable of crushing them to powder.

If the church at Ephesus needed love, the church at Smyrna needed to be prepared to face suffering and the church at Pergamum needed truth, then the church in Thyatira needed to discover God's burning, blazing holiness.

‹Make everything serve›

Christ's love for His people is such that He always commends them for their positive qualities before condemning them for their deficiencies. He says, "I know your deeds, your love and faith, your service and perseverance, and that you are now doing more than you did at first" (2:19). Not only did the church in Thyatira manifest the graces of love, faith, patience and service, but they were growing in those qualities week by week and month by month. While the church in Ephesus was backsliding, the church in Thyatira was moving ahead rapidly. As Christians, we never stand still – we are either moving forwards or backwards.

Some Christians complain that they are unable to grow in the Christian life because of their environment. But this simply is not true. The Christians in Thyatira were surrounded by hostility, contempt and ridicule, but they used the winds of adversity in the same way as an aircraft does – by taking advantage of the opposition, they rose to new heights of opportunity.

Someone said to me once, "You seem to repeat one statement over and over again in your writings: 'It's not so much what happens to you but what you do with it that matters.' Why do you do that?" I answered, "Because it has been an essential element in my growth in Christ and if you want to grow then it must be part of yours too." The statement is not mine, but the philosophy of life that it presents is part and parcel of my make-up and if you want to grow then it must become part of yours too. It's up to you to decide whether the place where you are or the people in your life will make you bitter – or better. You can use every impediment that comes to prod you towards growth and perfection. If you don't learn how to make your circumstances contribute to your faith, then your faith will soon become subservient to your circumstances.

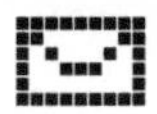

<A first-century Jezebel>

It comes as something of a shock to discover that in the midst of this beautiful garden – the church in Thyatira – a poisonous weed was beginning to appear: "Nevertheless, I have this against you: You tolerate that woman Jezebel, who calls herself a prophetess. By her teaching she misleads my servants into sexual immorality and the eating of food sacrificed to idols" (2:20). Although the church in Thyatira manifested clear evidences of the Christian life, holiness it seems was not one of them. It is this that Christ now bears down on, for He not only expects His Church to love Him, suffer for Him and uphold the truth for Him – He expects it also to be a holy Church, reflecting His purity and power to all around.

Obviously a woman who regarded herself as a prophetess was acting in a capacity similar to Jezebel, the wife of Ahab, whose conduct is described for us in the Old Testament (see 1 Kings 16:31–33; 18:4, 13; 19:1–2; 21). This disreputable woman had sought to contaminate Israel, as Balaam had done before her and now her spirit, so to speak, was at work in the Thyatiran church. The fruits flowering in the church were being blighted through sinful behaviour.

It needs holiness, as well as love, faith, patience and service, to make a church truly powerful. "The world cannot ignore a holy church," said W.E. Sangster. "The Church is not despised because it is holy. It is despised because it is not holy enough."

<The power of purity>

"The purpose of God for man," said one great Welsh theologian, "is not merely to make him happy, but to make him holy. Holiness first – happiness second." Some Christians might prefer to reverse this order, but to do so would be to tamper with the strategy of God, who seeks to impress upon us the necessity of purity as a commencement and bliss as a consequence.

In fact, with the New Testament open before us, it is hard to see why the subject of holiness is not more deeply emphasised in the Church's teaching and preaching at this present time. Over the past few decades something wonderful and significant has been happening in our ranks as a new stream of power flowed into the Church. There is evidence of great power in our midst as spiritual gifts appear, bringing blessing, encouragement and uplift. But is there the same evidence of purity? Thank God for all that is happening in the area of the gifts of the Spirit, but is it time that we gave equal attention to the fruit of the Spirit?

I believe with all my heart that God wants to quicken in us the desire for holiness. Nothing but an increase of holiness will make the Church the powerful force it should be in the world. This important quality is not to be regarded as the monopoly of the cloisters or the pet theme of certain branches of Christendom. It should be part and parcel of our daily living in the factory, the shop, the office, the hospital, school or home.

‹The patience of God›

The exalted Christ, whose eyes "are like blazing fire", now gazes into the darkness of the night which shrouded the sins of the esoteric group led by the self-styled prophetess, and pronounces the most severe warning: "I will cast her on a bed of suffering, and I will make those who commit adultery with her suffer intensely, unless they repent of her ways. I will strike her children dead ..." (2:22–23).

It would appear that a previous warning had been given to the woman who was the source of this deep problem in the church, for Christ says, "I have given her time to repent of her

immorality ..." (2:21). How infinitely patient God is, even with those who purposefully and deliberately violate His spiritual principles. Moreover, though Jezebel did not wish to repent – "but she is unwilling" (2:21) – the door of repentance was still left open for her followers, "unless they repent of her ways" (2:22). "He is patient with you," writes Peter, "not wanting anyone to perish, but everyone to come to repentance" (2 Pet. 3:9). The door of opportunity, however, will not be left open for too long, and Christ warns that unless there is evidence of their repentance soon, He will take the most serious action. Her bed of sin will become a bed of suffering.

This judgment on the prophetess, as well as that for her followers, is reminiscent of 1 Corinthians 11:30. In the judgment that fell upon the Corinthian church for their defilement of the Lord's Supper, some were weak and sick and others died. Let us be warned! But if we judge ourselves, then we shall not be judged (1 Cor. 11:31).

‹No greater burden›

One of Christ's most significant statements to the church in Thyatira is, "I will not impose any other burden on you" (2:24). This remark was addressed to those who had not been infected by the cancerous growth that had developed in the church: "... to you who do not hold to her teaching and have not learned Satan's so-called deep secrets" (2:24). Thankfully, there was a godly remnant in Thyatira who had not defiled themselves.

Commentators feel that this phrase is an unmistakable reference to a similar statement made by the apostles in their decree following the Jerusalem conference: "It seemed good to the Holy Spirit and to us not to burden you with anything beyond the following requirements ..." (Acts 15:28). The conclusion of that Jerusalem conference was, quite simply, that it was pointless to indulge in practices that were spiritually unnecessary. The point Christ is making in His letter to the Christians in Thyatira is that although they were surrounded by promiscuity and immorality, they were not to allow themselves to be pushed towards an extreme where their holiness became artificial and contrived. A new conflict with immorality must not drive them into a new asceticism.

Is this not His message to the Church today? Living as we do in an environment where moral standards are at an all-time low, we are not to think up some new remedy, but simply live out our lives in the power of the gospel – or, as Christ puts it – "Hold on to what you have until I come" (2:25).

<Our eternal reward>

As in all the seven letters, Christ concludes with a gracious promise to the overcomer. It is, in fact, twofold: "I will give authority over the nations"; and "I will also give him the morning star" (2:26–28).

The first promise borrows its tones from Psalm 2:8–9, where the Messiah's rule and authority over all things is foretold. This authority Christ now openly shares with His people. He is saying, in other words, "As I have received power from My Father, that power I now share with you." The promise is quite clearly intended to show the faithful remnant in Thyatira that submission to Christ's standards and obedience to His commands will one day entitle them to rule with Him on His throne. It is only as we submit to the standards of Christ's moral authority, that we ourselves can wield authority.

The second part of Christ's promise is, "I will also give him the morning star." What does this mean? Christ Himself is described

 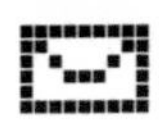

in Revelation as "the bright Morning Star" (22:16), so He is obviously promising them the gift of Himself. The Christian who rejects the darkness and misdeeds of Jezebel will discover instead the Morning Star. He will share not only in Christ's authority, but in Christ's glory. He will not only rule the universe alongside Christ, but will share in the Saviour's eternal splendour. He will actually possess Christ as well as being possessed by Him.

My friends, let us rejoice in this fact – no matter what we give up for Him down here on earth, it is nothing compared to the glory we shall share with Him when we see Him face to face.

⟨Further study⟩

Exod. 15:11; Psa. 99:1–9; Isa. 6:3; 1 Pet. 1:16

1. What did the cherubim declare?
2. What is Peter's exhortation?

Luke 1:74–75; 2 Cor 7:1; Heb. 12:14; 2 Pet. 3:1–11

3. What must we make every effort to do?
4. What will be the result?

Gal. 5:16; Eph. 4:1; Eph. 5:1–16; 1 John 1:7

5. What should characterise our life?
6. What is the wise way to live?

The_letter_to_the_church_at_Sardis, "The_Church_needs_life"_>>

Revelation 3:1–6

"To the angel of the church in Sardis write: These are the words of him who holds the seven spirits of God and the seven stars. ..."
(Revelation 3:1)

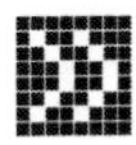

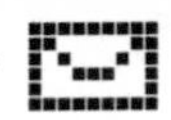

We come now to Christ's letter to the church in Sardis. This city lay about 50 miles east of Smyrna, and was a fairly busy centre of trade and traffic. Christ's first words to this church are once again related to the need and the condition of the local congregation. He describes Himself as the one who "holds the seven spirits of God and the seven stars". The seven stars present no problem to us as we know, from the first chapter, that these refer to the "angels" or presiding elders of the seven churches (1:20), but what meaning lies behind the strange expression, "seven spirits of God"?

The phrase, of course, is not new as this, too, appears in the first chapter: "from him who is, and who was, and who is to come, and from the seven spirits before his throne, and from Jesus Christ ..." (1:4–5). There is no doubt (to my mind, at least) that the reference here is to the Holy Spirit. "But," I hear you say, "I thought the Spirit was one, not seven." I am indebted to Archbishop Trench for a clear explanation of this statement, when he writes, "He [the Holy Spirit] is regarded here not so much in His personal unity, as His manifold energies." In other words, though the Holy Spirit is indeed one, He ministers to each of the seven churches at one and the same time.

We ask ourselves: Why does Christ begin by emphasising the ministry of His Spirit in this way? It is because the most urgent need of the church in Sardis was to experience the flow of the Spirit. Their need was not so much for love as for life.

<Christ's stringent test>

In this letter Christ departs from His characteristic manner of first commending before condemning, and swings immediately into a stern denunciation of the church: "I know your deeds; you have a reputation of being alive, but you are dead ... for I have not found your deeds complete in the sight of my God" (3:1–2). The church in Sardis had gained a reputation throughout the whole of Asia Minor for being a progressive and lively centre of Christian witness. But outward appearances are deceptive and the truth was that the church was nothing more than a spiritual graveyard. It had a name for being alive, but in actual fact it was dead. They had an endless round of spiritual activity but, like the church in Ephesus, in the sight of Christ they were beggared, bankrupt and broken.

Surely this is a word that speaks right into the need of many local congregations today. Billy Graham often asks congregations this pointed question: "If you were arrested for being a Christian, would there be enough evidence to convict you?" The tragedy is that we can pass the tests of men and come up with a lifestyle that they would regard as decidedly Christian, yet when brought before the bar of Christ, we would be judged as wanting.

The church in Sardis would have passed the test of men, but it failed the test of Christ. Listen again to His words: "I have not found your deeds complete in the sight of my God." Is it possible that there are churches in the twenty-first century whose social projects, fashionable clothes and endless activity, are just the disguise of an ecclesiastical corpse?

⟨More than a name⟩

A church may have a wide variety of human talent, a good deal of money, manpower and prestige, but if it lacks the vital flow of the Spirit, then it is nothing more than a spiritual graveyard.

Samuel Chadwick, in his book *The Way to Pentecost* writes, "The Church is helpless without the presence and power of the Spirit. The lust for talk about work increases as the power declines. Conferences multiply when work fails. We are acting as

 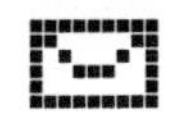

though the only remedy for decline were method, organisation and compromise. The helplessness of the Church is pathetic and tragic. There might be no such Person as the Holy Ghost."

Of course, since Samuel Chadwick wrote those words, the Church has moved into a wider understanding of the Spirit's indispensability but, nonetheless, there are still far too many Christian congregations who excel in the mechanics and fail in the dynamics. The Church that is managed by men and not governed by the Holy Spirit is doomed to failure. Men and women can, of course, supply the energy, the enterprise for things that are human, but the real ministry and effectiveness of a Christian church depends upon the flow of the Spirit in its midst. Religious services, reciting the creed or even singing hymns and worship songs, do not constitute a Christian church. A true Christian church exists when people carry God in their hearts, and not upon their backs.

⟨True worship⟩

The church in Sardis needed to experience the life-giving flow of the Spirit that would turn their dull routines into radiant and exciting acts of Christian worship. What can be worse than ceremony without life? We can have a fine choir, an elegant church building, a fashionable congregation who sing the hymns and chant the creeds with dignity and excellence, but if there is no flow of the Holy Spirit in those acts, then the words will rise no higher than the roof.

A young man told of having a dream one night in which he saw himself in heaven looking down on the congregation in which he usually worshipped. He saw them stand to sing at the invitation of the minister and, to his surprise, even though he saw their mouths opening, no sound floated up to his ears. Then he heard just one voice, the voice of an old lady sitting in the corner of the church, so, turning to an angel standing nearby, he asked the reason. "Out of all that goes on in that church," said the angel, "only true acts of worship rise up here to heaven. That old lady is the only one whose heart is in her act of worship – and so that is the only voice that gets through."

One well-known minister, in commenting upon this situation of mere ceremony without life, says, "We can lead the prayers in such a perfunctory manner that the congregation never reach the Throne of Grace, and we can preach to display our learning more than to exalt Christ and bring glory to Him."

If our worship is to rise higher than the roofs of our churches, then it must be worship that is Spirit-inspired and Spirit-directed.

‹Is yours a "dead church"?›

And what is the remedy Christ proposes to the situation in the church at Sardis? "Wake up! Strengthen what remains and is about to die, for I have not found your deeds complete in the sight of my God. Remember, therefore, what you have received and heard; obey it, and repent" (3:2–3).

It is encouraging to see that not everyone in Sardis was suffering from the general decay. A minority were unaffected by the moribund condition of the general congregation and these, who were loyal to Jesus, formed a godly remnant whom Christ now commends. God has so often brought about great changes in His Church through minorities. A small group of people in a church where there is a great deal of pageantry and ceremony but no life can, under God, bring about spiritual revolution and change. Are you in what is termed "a dead church", and wonder whether you should get out and go elsewhere? Well, hold on a little longer and meet with the few other "live" Christians in the

church to pray and believe that God will yet break through in power and glory in your midst. A sincere, believing remnant can strengthen what remains, and be the means in God's hands of a major spiritual awakening.

The Sardian church was told also to remember and repent. "The shortest route to repentance," said someone, "is remembrance." Remember how it used to be and let the memory lead you to personal and corporate repentance. Who knows but that the action of allowing past history to challenge you to a new commitment, will be used by God to bring a new spiritual awakening in your church.

⟨"Be filled with the Spirit"⟩

Did the church in Sardis respond to the moving appeal of Christ to remember, repent and return? We will never really know what effect Christ's words had upon that local congregation until we arrive in eternity, but what is more important is that right now we make sure, each one of us, that His message to us does not go unheeded. To have a name among men that we are alive in Christ is not enough. We must make sure that we pass the tests of Christ by opening ourselves to the life-giving flow of the Spirit and obeying His command given to us in Ephesians 5:18: "Be filled with the Spirit."

We have said before that unless we daily open ourselves to the Holy Spirit, and know that constant day by day inflowing of the Spirit in our personal lives and our corporate worship, then we are disobedient Christians. Ephesians 5:18 is, as C.H. Spurgeon said, "not just a promise to be enjoyed, but a command to be obeyed". We must neither soil our garments (3:4) nor betray our name. Filled with the Holy Spirit and surrendered to Him, we can conquer and overcome every device of the devil to reduce our effectiveness and bring us into spiritual inertia.

The Church is the creation of the Holy Spirit. It is a group of believers who owe their spiritual life to Him, and apart from the Spirit there can be neither a Christian nor a church. Let us open ourselves to His Spirit so that, as in Ezekiel's vision, the breath of the four winds will blow and turn death into life and dry bones into mighty armies (Ezek. 37).

<He confesses us>

The letter to Sardis ends with a promise to the overcomer, once again appropriate to the need and condition of the church. Again the promise is twofold: "He who overcomes will ... be dressed in white"; and "I will never blot out his name from the book of life" (3:5). White is a popular colour in the book of Revelation and while it can symbolise many things (such as festivity and victory) its main use in Scripture is to symbolise purity. It was obvious that some in Sardis had soiled their garments (3:4) by allowing themselves to be involved in religious ceremony where there was no life. But those who resisted the temptation to externalise their faith, hanging it on the pegs of rituals and ceremonies, would one day be dressed in white and enjoy an eternal fellowship with Christ in heaven: "They will walk with me" (3:4).

The second promise is that their names should not be blotted out of the book of life. Can I ask you if your name is written in the Lamb's book of life? You can have the name of being spiritually alive (like the church in Sardis) and yet not be enrolled in the book of life. Your name can only be inscribed there when you surrender yourself fully to Christ, repent of sin and let Him save you by His grace. Christ's promise to the conquerors is that He will not blot out their names (3:5). The Greek sentence has a double negative which really says, "I will

 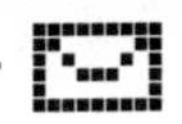

never, by any means, blot out his name." But there is more, "but will acknowledge his name before my Father and his angels" (3:5). He promises not merely to retain your name, but confess it before His Father and the angels. What a wonderful Saviour!

⟨Further study⟩

2 Cor. 3:17; 1 John 3:24, 4:13

1. What does the Spirit of the Lord bring?
2. What does the Spirit cause us to know?

Acts 13:2; 16:1–15; Rom. 8:14

3. What was the experience of the Early Church?
4. Is it your experience also?

John 6:63; Rom. 8:1–11; 2 Cor. 3:6; 1 Pet. 3:18

5. What does the Spirit give?
6. How does this relate to Christ's resurrection?

The_letter_to_the_church_at Philadelphia,_"He_has_the_keys"_>>

Revelation 3:7–13

"To the angel of the church in Philadelphia write: These are the words of him who is holy and true, who holds the key of David. ..."
(Revelation 3:7)

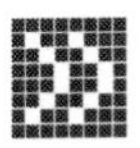

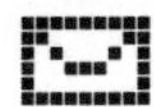

We continue following our imaginary postman on his journey and we come now to the sixth of these churches – the church in Philadelphia. The town of Philadelphia was situated about 35 miles south-east of Sardis in what was known to be a dangerously volcanic area, and Strabo called Philadelphia "a city full of earthquakes". Despite its dangerous situation, however, there existed within it a thriving community of God's people – a church which received almost unqualified commendation from our Lord Jesus Christ.

Before commending the church for its loyalty and devotion, Christ begins in the style which we have come to expect in these seven letters, by revealing Himself in a distinctive manner. In this case, He says He is the one who is "holy and true, who holds the key of David. What he opens no-one can shut, and what he shuts no-one can open" (3:7).

In addition to revealing Himself as holy and true, Christ claims to possess the key of David. The figure is doubtless borrowed from Isaiah 22:22: "I will place on his shoulder the key to the house of David; what he opens no-one can shut, and what he shuts no-one can open" where it is used of Eliakim, one of three delegates chosen to negotiate with Rabshakeh for the kingdom of Judah.

Christ reminds the church at Philadelphia that the doors of opportunity are completely under His control. If He wants them open, no one can shut them. If He wants them shut, no one can open them. He alone has the key.

⟨The open door⟩

While the church in Sardis received almost unmitigated condemnation, the church in Philadelphia received almost unqualified praise: "I know your deeds. See, I have placed before you an open door that no-one can shut" (3:8). What is this "open door" of which Christ speaks? There can be no doubt it is the door of Christian service. Once we come to Christ through the open door of salvation, our eyes fall upon another open door – the door of service. The opportunities open to the church in Philadelphia for sharing their faith were tremendous. The Holy Spirit was at work stirring the minds of men and women and creating within their hearts a thirst for the water of life.

When we examine the details surrounding this church, however, we could, if we wanted to, make out a strong argument as to why they should not have to actively share their faith. They were not a strong congregation in size or influence – "I know that you have little strength" (3:8). Moreover, the opposition to them from the local group of Jewish people was so fanatical that Christ calls them "the synagogue of Satan". Then a third reason, perhaps, why they should not move out was the impending threat of persecution (3:10).

Three good reasons why they should dig their heels in and stay as they were. But what does Christ command? He admonishes them to walk through the open door under His banner and, despite their weakness, He promises that some of their converts will include those who were the fiercest antagonists (3:9).

⟨A wide open door⟩

William Ramsay, in his book *The Letters to the Seven Churches of Asia*, claims that when the city was founded in the second-century BC, it was designed to be a strategic centre for the spreading of the Greek language throughout the whole of Asia. "It was," says Professor Ramsay, "a missionary city from the beginning."

Whatever the city may have been for Greek culture, it was now to be a springboard for the propagation of the Christian faith. Standing as it did on the borders of Mysia, Lydia and Phrygia, it

was, as someone described it, "like an archer's bow ready to thrust its arrows deep into the heart of the interior". The Philadelphian church had the glorious opportunity to spread far and wide the wonderful news of the grace of God. The door was open. No man could shut it.

The same is true of the Christian Church at this momentous hour. It is true, of course, that some doors are closed but many are open. While great difficulties exist for the traditional missionary approach to some countries of the world there are, on the other hand, wide open doors for competent, trained and qualified men and women, committed to Jesus Christ, to work as nurses, doctors, scientists, industrialists, technicians, engineers, etc.

‹The will to evangelise›

All around us God is moving in the hearts of men and women, creating within them a longing for reality, and each group of believers must be aware of this and think and pray through the best ways in which their local area can be evangelised. Not all areas respond to the same kind of approach. One thing, however, is sure – every church must have the will to evangelise, and where before the desire to evangelise has been in our minds and in our emotions; now it must get into our will. We must decide to share with others what has been shared with us.

Mark Guy Pearce spoke right to the heart of the matter when he said, "Unless a man's faith saves him out of selfishness into service, it will certainly never save him out of hell into heaven." If we wait for some kind of emotion to overtake us and send us out as blazing evangelists to the community around, then we might wait a lifetime. The truth is this: The Christian believer, or church, which has received from Christ an assurance of salvation, is commanded to share that message with all who live around – continually, clearly and convincingly.

Having come in through the door of salvation, we hurry out through the door of service to look for others and attempt, in the words of our Lord Jesus Christ, to "make them come in" (Luke 14:23). We must decide to share with others what God has decided to share with us.

<Interferers – or interpreters>

Without realising it, when we fail to evangelise, we interfere with the purposes of Christ. When people brought their children to Jesus it was said that the disciples "interfered" (Mark 10:13, Weymouth). They tried to keep the little children away and in doing so interfered with the spirit and the purpose of Christ. You and I have the opportunity to be either interferers or interpreters of Christ. Which is it to be?

I have used a good many interpreters on my overseas assignments; some have augmented the message and others have detracted from it. Imagine my surprise when, in one country, my appointed interpreter shook my hand and said, "I am your interrupter." In Madras, South India, I was told, "Your interpreter is so good that whatever you say, and however you say it, he will see that it is understood by the audience – exactly the way you say it." In working with that interpreter, I felt such unity and harmony that it was almost like being mentally and spiritually one with him.

Sometimes, however, an interpreter can block the message either by being in it too much or not being in it at all. Is this our problem when it comes to sharing our Christian faith? Are we perfunctory? Does the message consume us? Do we burn with it? Each one of us must face the challenge that comes to our hearts by the Spirit today: Do we truly interpret Him? Are we

interrupters – or true interpreters?

⟨Going with the gospel⟩

It is important to recognise that Christ's words were not addressed to an individual, it was before the whole church in Philadelphia that Christ had opened a door. This is, indeed, the New Testament vision and ideal. Evangelism is not just the task of a selected few; it is Christ's commission to the whole Church. It is true that some may not be perfectly suited to face-to-face confrontation with the unconverted, but they can be involved at some other level. The important thing is that the whole Church is involved in a corporate effort to evangelise.

How much impact is your local church making on its neighbourhood? Is your congregation being trained and prepared for a corporate offensive in taking the gospel into the homes, hospitals, factories, schools, colleges, shops and offices in your community? Is a clear plan being developed to mobilise your forces and prepare everyone for their place in this spiritual offensive?

Every local church must, of course, think and pray through its own special approach to its own particular neighbourhood and community. It must not carbon-copy the methods used by another church in another setting. Don't barge your way unceremoniously through locked doors. If some doors remain shut, don't put your shoulder to them. Wait until Christ takes out His key and opens them. Some doors, of course, will fly open and it is through them that you must enter. Remain sensitive to God's leading and to the guidance of His Spirit and your evangelism will be effective and productive.

‹A pillar in His temple›

Christ once again closes His letter with a promise to the conqueror and overcomer: “I am coming soon. Hold on to what you have, so that no-one will take your crown” (3:11). Then comes His special pledge: “Him who overcomes I will make a pillar in the temple of my God. Never again will he leave it. I will write on him the name of my God and the name of the city of my God, the new Jerusalem ... and I will also write on him my new name” (3:12).

What could be more appropriate and relevant to the Christians in Philadelphia? And, indeed, what could be more appropriate to those of us in the Church at this present time? If we renounce a life of indolence and indifference and dare to enter through the door of service, we will gain the security of being a pillar in the Paradise of God. If we lay down our names for Him in this world, then in the next we will take up a new name. The Philadelphian Christians might, indeed, live in fear of sudden and violent earthquakes, but they were given the promise that nothing could or would disturb them when they found themselves as pillars in God’s heaven. The open door stands for opportunity and evangelism; the key of David stands for Christ’s authority and sovereignty; the pillars for the believer’s security.

Do we hear the appeal of Christ at this urgent hour? He holds open the doors of exciting service. May every one of His churches know the joy of leading men and women in through the door of salvation and out through the doors of service.

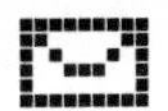

⟨Further study⟩

Rom. 10:1, 11:14; 1 Cor. 9:22–23; 2 Cor. 5:10–21

1. What compelled Paul?
2. What was Paul's desire?

Matt. 24:14; Matt. 28:19; Mark 16:12–18; Luke 24:36–49

3. What was Christ's great commission?
4. How are you fulfilling it?

Luke 2:25; Acts 2:3; 8:17; 10:34–48; 19:6

5. What happened while Peter preached?
6. When did this last happen in your church?

The_letter_to_the_church_at Laodicea,_"The_Church_without _the_Spirit"_>>

Revelation 3:14–22

"To the angel of the church in Laodicea write: These are the words of the Amen, the faithful and true witness..."
(Revelation 3:14)

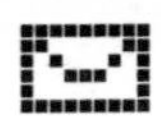

As we come to the last of the seven churches of Asia, it might be helpful to remind ourselves of each of the distinctive characteristics of the six churches we have looked at so far.

The Ephesian Christians were urged to return to their first love, while the believers in Smyrna were warned that their uncompromising stand would inevitably lead to unrelieved suffering. The church in Pergamum was commanded to uphold the truth in the face of the most grievous error and the church in Thyatira bidden to pursue holiness and righteousness. In Sardis, the need was for life, and true life of the Spirit without which religion becomes a mere ritual, while in Philadelphia the need was for the church to pass through the open doors of opportunity and service that lay before them in bringing the gospel to Mysia, Lydia and Phrygia.

Now Christ addresses Himself to the church in Laodicea, a city about 45 miles south-east of Philadelphia and the most southerly of the seven cities. The church there had lapsed into a state of lukewarmness, and this condition brings from the lips of Christ the sternest of rebukes and the most severe condemnation. The need of the Laodicean church was undoubtedly to open themselves to the flow of the Holy Spirit, without which the Church is a mere shell.

We know that apart from the Holy Spirit there can be no Christianity and no Church. Worship is idolatry unless the Spirit flows through it. No local church can live up to Christ's expectations unless it gives room for the Spirit to work in its midst.

‹The divine Yes›

We have seen in each letter that Christ reveals Himself to the church in the way that is most appropriate to their need. Here He announces Himself as "the Amen, the faithful and true witness" (3:14). The Hebrew word *Amen* means "verily" or "indeed", a word of assent. It means much more than Christ merely saying "Amen". It means that He is the Amen. Moffatt translates 2 Corinthians 1:20 thus: "The divine 'yes' has ... sounded in Him." All of God's character is seen in Christ and when He speaks, He speaks for God because He is God. He is not just an Amen tagged on to what God says – what Christ says, God says and what God says, Christ says. Because of this, His words are true and trustworthy, hence He is "the faithful and true witness". Dr E.S. Jones says, "Jesus is God's 'Yes' to all the promises the Almighty has ever made."

He is also described as "the beginning of the creation of God" (3:14, Phillips). The word translated "beginning" ("ruler", NIV), has been pounced upon by Jehovah's Witnesses and others in an attempt to prove that Christ was created by God and is, therefore, not God's equal. However, the phrase actually means that Christ is the originator of God's creation. As Colossians 1:16 says, "for by him all things were created". Christ is the "uncreated principle of creation" out of whom flowed the whole of God's creation.

How can we ignore the very Being who gave us existence? He knows everything about us and yet His knowledge of our secret sins does not block the stream of His love. He is not against us for our sin, but for us against our sin.

⟨Nauseating Christians⟩

Christ begins His stern indictment of the Laodicean church by characteristically informing them that He knows all about their spiritual need – which is that they are neither cold nor hot (3:15). The Greek words carry the meaning of icily cold and boiling hot. The Laodiceans were lukewarm Christians who had

 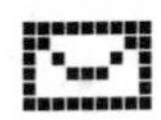

allowed their zeal to lapse into a state of half-heartedness. Professor H.B. Swete believes that this phrase has "an allusion to the hot springs of Hierapolis, which, in their way over the plateau, became lukewarm, and in this condition discharged themselves over the cliff right opposite to Laodicea". The Laodicean church was like a lukewarm waterfall giving no refreshment to those who stood beneath its flow.

The message to the church in Laodicea is quite plain: " ... because you are lukewarm – neither hot nor cold – I am about to spit you out of my mouth" (3:16). Jesus Christ would prefer His people to be either frozen or on fire. There is no in-between. He says quite categorically that if we are not going to be hot, then He would prefer us to be cold – not lukewarm (3:15).

Why is this? The meaning is not hard to discover. If Christ is truly the Son of God who died on Calvary and rose again on the third day, then only a radiant faith can truly represent those facts. A mere lukewarm appreciation simply detracts from their real meaning and confuses those who look on. Better icy indifference or even active opposition than to insult Him by saying we believe in His cause while living out lives that, by their indifference, nauseate His very Being.

<The cure for complacency>

If you are offended by the strong language Christ uses here, then pause to consider the reason for it.

The root cause of lukewarmness is complacency. And how do you get people out of complacency? By shocking them out of it! A lukewarm Christian is blind to his own condition. He sees one thing and does another. The only way he can be delivered is by penetrating his defences with barbed words that open up his soul and reveal the reality of his condition. Are you ready to be shocked? Then read on, for this is precisely what Christ proceeds to do to the Laodicean Christians: "You say, 'I am rich; I have acquired wealth and do not need a thing.' But you do not realise that you are wretched, pitiful, poor, blind and naked" (3:17).

Laodicea was known throughout the whole of Asia for its material prosperity. The city was a mercantile banking centre. A famous school existed there connected with the Temple of Asklepios whose physicians prepared a special ointment for the cure of ophthalmia. In addition to this, they were expert in the manufacture of cloth and special garments. The citizens of Laodicea were proud of their achievements. Had this spirit crept into Christ's church? Yes. They were smug, complacent and self-satisfied. They thought they were fine but, in fact, Christ describes them as blind and naked beggars.

‹Fan into flame›

We need to be one thing or the other in our Christian experience – cold or hot. Does the idea of being on fire for Christ hint of emotionalism? Does it conjure up in your mind fanatical scenes in which the heart runs away with the head? Paul told his followers in Romans 12:11: "… keep your spiritual fervour" – a phrase which really means "keep boiling hot", and to Timothy he said, "… fan into flame the gift of God, which is in you ..." (2 Tim. 1:6). Many of us, if we are honest, will have to confess that we are scared stiff of enthusiasm, yet it is something of which Christ approves. "Be zealous and repent," is His command to the Laodiceans (3:19, NKJ).

Consider the record of church history. Whenever the fount of living water breaks forth fresh from the rock, it flows with power and enthusiasm. The first Christians were accused of being drunk (Acts 2:13) – an accusation from which we are far

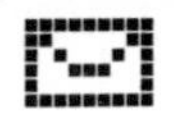

removed. But how strange it is that when the river has been running for some time it tends to slow down and enthusiasm wanes. Dr W.E. Sangster in his book *These Things Abide* says, "Exuberance and devotion can belong together. It is when the fires in individual hearts or denominations are dying down that convention frowns on exuberance, and an air of superiority is affected towards those who cannot restrain the primitive joy."

Enthusiasm is an essential and important part of Christianity and without it the Christian faith becomes dry and mechanical. Perhaps if we were to live nearer to the heart of our faith we too might be accused, as were the early disciples, of being "drunk and mad".

<The wonderful Counsellor>

The Christians in Laodicea were caught up in a spirit of complacency, so much so that despite their wealth they were beggars, despite their medical schools they were blind and despite their clothing factories they were naked. This is Christ's diagnosis of a lukewarm Christian. Dare we turn away from it? To ignore the advice of a skilled physician is to court disaster. We may flatter ourselves that we are fine, but our risen Lord, whose eyes burn with fire, penetrates the deepest recesses of our being and sees us exactly as we are.

Now that Christ has pinpointed the cause of their problem, He proceeds to give the cure: "I counsel you to buy from me gold refined in the fire ... and white clothes to wear ... and salve to put on your eyes" (3:18).What a wonderful counsellor is our Lord Jesus Christ. He is, in fact, the only counsellor in the whole universe who doesn't need counselling Himself. He has the right to issue a strong command to the Christians in Laodicea, but instead He tenderly appeals to them to listen to His words: "I counsel you". It is because He loves us, that He rebukes us (3:19). There is no personal spite or malice in His words, but infinite tenderness, compassion and consideration. He has welcome news for beggars. They are spiritually poor, but Christ is rich. They are naked, but Christ has the wherewithal to clothe their nakedness. They are blind, but He has the eye salve to heal their blindness.

How can this come about? They must "be earnest and repent" (3:19). When they are ready to spit complacency out of their mouths, then they will have the assurance that Christ will not spit them out of His.

‹If anyone ...›

When Christ says, "To him who overcomes, I will give the right to sit with me on my throne" (3:21), His words are not, as is often supposed, an appeal to the whole church in Laodicea. They are intensely personal. "If anyone ..." He says in verse 20. The church may not act as a corporate body in repenting and recapturing their zeal, but if any one of the members will show a spirit of repentance, then Christ will enter into his or her spiritual experience to bring an end to the poverty.

In these beautiful words Christ likens the human heart to a dwelling. Each one of us has the right, if we so wish, to refuse admission to the very God who made us. He will not break down the door. He will stand and knock ... and knock again, appealing for our permission to enter so that He can bring with Him the resources to end our poverty. If we open our hearts to Him, then we have the promise of sitting with Him on His throne. "To him who overcomes, I will give the right to sit with me on my throne" (3:21). When we bow before His throne here on earth and submit to His lordship and sovereignty, then we finish up with Him on His throne in eternity. If we let Christ enter through the

door of our lives, then He will let us enter into the house of His Father. If we allow Him to sit with us at our table, He will allow us to sit with Him at His.

Here, then, is the challenge. To be half-hearted is so distasteful to Christ that it nauseates Him. We must either throw the door of our lives wide open to Him or firmly slam it shut in His face. There must be no prevarication. "He who has an ear, let him hear what the Spirit says to the churches" (3:22).

⟨Further study⟩

Isa. 6:1–9; Matt. 3:11; Heb. 12:29

1. What made an impact on Isaiah's life?
2. What was John the Baptist's declaration?

Psa. 41:1–4; Jer. 3:22; Hos. 6:1

3. What was the psalmist's prayer?
4. What did Hosea exhort?

John 17:1–23; Gal. 2:20; Eph. 3:17–18

5. What was Jesus' prayer?
6. What was Paul's testimony?

Our_God_reigns_>>

Revelation 4:1–11; 5:1–14

"... and there before me was a throne in heaven with someone sitting on it."
(Revelation 4:2)

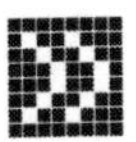

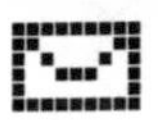

Now that we have considered the qualities which Christ expects of His Church, namely love, readiness to suffer for Him, truth, holiness, reality, service and zealousness, we must turn our attention from the Church on earth to the Church in heaven.

Most commentators believe that the sentence, "After this I looked, and there before me was a door standing open in heaven" (4:1) refers to the transition of the Church from its ministry on earth to its destiny in heaven. The flickering candles now give way to the rainbow-encircled throne: "and there before me was a throne in heaven with someone sitting on it" (4:2). It is perhaps difficult to imagine the effect that this vision of the rainbow-encircled throne would have on those early Christians living as they did in the midst of persecution and tribulation. Yet let's see if we can think our way into their circumstances so that we might feel something of it.

The churches in Asia were surrounded by hostility, suspicion and distrust. They lived from day to day under the threat of fierce persecution and death. At any time an imperial edict could be issued to wipe them off the face of the earth. How does God support His people at such times? He gives them a vision of His throne. From this throne the great galaxies of the universe receive their orders enabling them to keep their precision and accuracy. Before it, all creatures must finally bow.

The vision that sustained those early Christians is the one that will also sustain us. Hallelujah! Our God reigns.

⟨Why a throne?⟩

In your study of the Scriptures, have you noticed that the seers and the apostles in their times of deepest perplexity were often sustained and supported by a vision of the heavenly throne? In the year that King Uzziah died, the prophet Isaiah saw the Lord "seated on a throne" (Isa. 6:1). When Ezekiel sustained the forlorn exiles by his prophecies and predictions, he was given a vision of the eternal throne (Ezek. 1:26). When Daniel pronounced the details of the abomination of desolation, he saw a throne (Dan. 7:9–10). Why a throne – God's throne? By this vision God wants to reassure His people that the universe is His, and no matter what happens on earth, the ultimate and final seat of authority is in the heavens. A monarch reigns from his throne. It is the symbol of authority.

I realise that to those early Christians it looked (as indeed it may appear to you at this moment) as if the world was anything but firmly in God's grip. Murder, greed, lust, selfishness, pride, jealousy spread across the face of the earth, and the powers of darkness seemed to be closing in on those small churches in Asia, yet the sight of God's throne strengthened them to go on and partly sustained them in the hour of overwhelming trial. May it be the same in our experience as we gaze upon it right now.

‹Can God feel?›

Why was the vision of the eternal throne partly responsible for sustaining and supporting those early Christians in the seven churches of Asia? Because it was not just the vision of the throne that sustained them, but also the One who sat upon it: "Then I saw a Lamb, looking as if it had been slain, standing in the centre of the throne ..."(5:6). Just think of it – Christ, the sinless, spotless, Lamb of God occupies the eternal throne.

Some theologians have written about what they term "the impassivity of God". "God can't feel," they say. "How can the Supreme Being of the great universe be troubled by our trifling sorrows and transient pains?" We might believe them had we not seen that great God, in Jesus Christ His Son, suffering on the cross. No, the idea that God has no feelings is a libel on the character of the God we love. Incarnation added to the experience of God and brought Him to suffer and die on the cross. As the author of Hebrews explained, He has learned many things by His sufferings (Heb. 5:8). And what suffering He endured – the pain of being misunderstood by His disciples; the agony of the Garden when, with torturing slowness, it seemed that the end would never come (remember His words to Judas: "What you are about to do, do quickly" – or, as one translator puts it: "Get it over with" [John 13:27]); the cruel nails of the cross; the pain and the shame and the ignominy!

It is all over now. On the throne of God in heaven our sympathising Saviour appears. He knows our weakness, has borne our pains and sorrows and His presence on the throne is proof that He not only knows – but cares.

‹Brought to His feet!›

The presence of Christ on that eternal throne is proof that our humanity is in heaven, and that God feels for us with a sensitivity way beyond our own.

> The dear token of His passion
> Still His dazzling body bears. (*Charles Wesley*)

Scientists, we are told, are able to study the chemistry on other planets. They claim that there is just one chemistry of the heavenly bodies: that oxygen is still oxygen on Venus, and nitrogen is still nitrogen on Mars. All the feelings God experienced on earth through the sufferings of His Son have been carried back onto the throne, and they are not only found there in all their fullness, but will remain so throughout all eternity. The vision of Christ, the suffering Lamb with open wounds – "as if it had been slain" (5:6) – is proof that He still carries on His body "the dear tokens of His passion". Christ has bridged the gulf and carried our humanity back into glory.

Do you remember when Stephen made his defence before the Sanhedrin, and brought upon himself capital punishment? Just before his death, he said: "I see heaven open and the Son of Man standing ..." (Acts 7:56). Standing? But surely Christ is seated at the right hand of God (Heb. 1:3)? He is – but Stephen's death brought the Son of God to His feet in a demonstration of infinite compassion and love.

‹Even so, come, Lord Jesus›

As we end our studies on the subject of "What Christ expects of His Church", let's try to focus on some of the more salient things we have been saying. We have seen quite clearly the qualities and marks which Christ wants to see in His redeemed people – a passionate love, a willingness to suffer, truth of doctrine, holiness of life, inward reality, a sharing of our faith and zealousness of service. And how can all these qualities be supported and sustained? It is by the vision of our risen Lord seated upon the eternal throne! Given this, we can face anything.

The book of Revelation leaves us with no doubt that the Lord God omnipotent reigns. The destiny of the ages is in the hands of our Saviour, Jesus Christ. Nothing can proceed without first receiving His permission and approval. All that will happen can only happen because He allows it. The winds of persecution are controlled by Him, and He only allows what He can use. No matter what comes, the Church's security is guaranteed by God the Father, God the Son and God the Holy Spirit.

Our studies on the Church have now come to an end but the Church itself lives on. And how! The Christian Church will triumph over all things – even the grave. Did you realise that the Church is the only society in the world that never loses a member by death? With our eyes on the eternal throne, we can face anything that comes and one day soon the King of the universe will give us shelter on that throne, where we shall gaze upon Him and worship Him throughout the unending ages of eternity.

⟨Further study⟩

Isa. 53:1–7; John 1:29; 1 Pet. 1:18–19; Rev. 13:8

1. What did Isaiah prophesy?
2. What did John declare?

Psa. 123:1; Acts 1:10; Acts 7; 1 Cor. 13:12; 1 John 3:2

3. What is the hope of every believer?
4. What does it seem like at the present?

Acts 2:46–47, 5:14, 6:7; 11:11–24

5. What picture do we get of the Early Church?
6. Is it the same in your church?

‹NATIONAL DISTRIBUTORS›

UK: (and countries not listed below)
CWR, Waverley Abbey House, Waverley Lane, Farnham, Surrey GU9 8EP.
Tel: (01252) 784710
Outside UK (44) 1252 784710

AUSTRALIA: CMC Australasia, PO Box 519, Belmont, Victoria 3216. Tel: (03) 5241 3288

CANADA: CMC Distribution Ltd, PO Box 7000, Niagara on the Lake, Ontario L0S 1J0. Tel: (0800) 325 1297

GHANA: Challenge Enterprises of Ghana, PO Box 5723, Accra. Tel: (021) 222437/223249 Fax: (021) 226227

HONG KONG: Cross Communications Ltd, 1/F, 562A Nathan Road, Kowloon. Tel: 2780 1188 Fax: 2770 6229

INDIA: Crystal Communications, 10-3-18/4/1, East Marredpally, Secunderabad – 500 026. Tel/Fax: (040) 7732801

KENYA: Keswick Bookshop, PO Box 10242, Nairobi. Tel: (02) 331692/226047

MALAYSIA: Salvation Book Centre (M) Sdn Bhd, 23 Jalan SS 2/64, 47300 Petaling Jaya, Selangor. Tel: (03) 78766411/78766797 Fax: (03) 78757066/78756360

NEW ZEALAND: CMC New Zealand Ltd, Private Bag, 17910 Green Lane, Auckland. Tel: (09) 5249393 Fax: (09) 5222137

NIGERIA: FBFM, Helen Baugh House, 96 St Finbarr's College Road, Akoka, Lagos. Tel: (01) 7747429/4700218/825775/827264

PHILIPPINES: OMF Literature Inc, 776 Boni Avenue, Mandaluyong City. Tel: (02) 531 2183 Fax: (02) 531 1960

REPUBLIC OF IRELAND: Scripture Union, 40 Talbot Street, Dublin 1. Tel: (01) 8363764

SINGAPORE: Campus Crusade Asia Ltd, 315 Outram Road, 06-08 Tan Boon Liat Building, Singapore 169074. Tel: (065) 222 3640

SOUTH AFRICA: Struik Christian Books, 80 MacKenzie Street, PO Box 1144, Cape Town 8000. Tel: (021) 462 4360 Fax: (021) 461 3612

SRI LANKA: Christombu Books, 27 Hospital Street, Colombo 1. Tel: (01) 433142/328909

TANZANIA: CLC Christian Book Centre, PO Box 1384, Mkwepu Street, Dar es Salaam. Tel: (051) 2119439

UGANDA: New Day Bookshop, PO Box 2021, Kampala. Tel: (041) 255377

ZIMBABWE: Word of Life Books, Shop 4, Memorial Building, 35 S Machel Avenue, Harare. Tel: (04) 781305 Fax: (04) 774739

For e-mail addresses, visit the CWR web site: www.cwr.org.uk

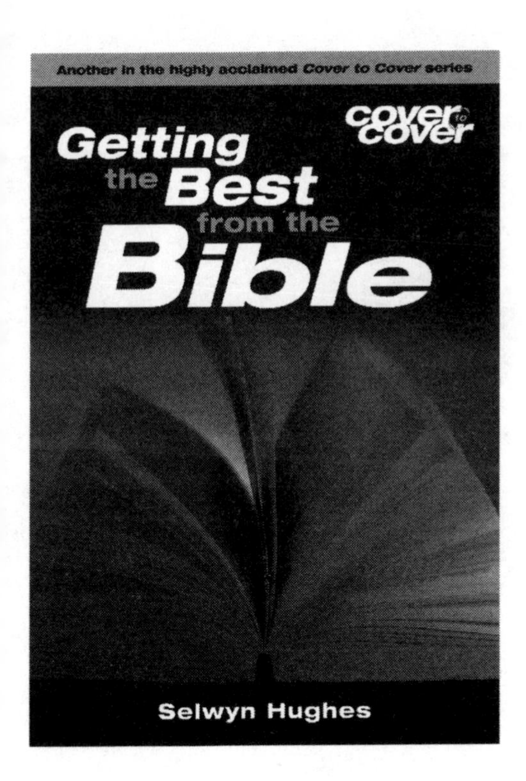

Getting_the_Best_from_the_Bible>>

Realise the full potential of God's Word in your life. *Getting the Best from the Bible* is part of the *Cover to Cover* series and combines inspired, insightful writing with helpful practical guides. This essential book takes a new look at ways to illuminate God's Word and reveals how to apply Bible principles to everyday life.

Price: **£4.99**

ISBN: 1–85345–187–8

God's
People